The United States: Historical Atlases of the Growth of a New Nation ™

A HISTORICAL ATLAS OF
America's Manifest Destiny

Lesli J. Favor, Ph.D.

The Rosen Publishing Group, Inc., New York

For Loyd and June Anderson, Oklahoma farmers for over fifty years.

Published in 2005 by The Rosen Publishing Group, Inc.
29 East 21st Street, New York, NY 10010

First Edition

Library of Congress Cataloging-in-Publication Data

Favor, Lesli J.
A historical atlas of America's manifest destiny/Lesli J. Favor.
    p. cm. — (The United States: historical atlases of the growth of a new nation)
Includes bibliographical references and (p. 62) index.
Contents: Claiming the west — Pushing westward — New territories — Blazing trails — Fighting over slavery — Settling the west — The end of an era.
ISBN 1-4042-0201-3
1. United States — Territorial expansion — Juvenile literature. 2. West (U.S.) — History — Juvenile Literature. 3. Frontier and pioneer life — West (U.S.) — Juvenile literature. 4. United States — Territorial expansion — Maps for children. 5. West (U.S) — History — Maps for children. 6. Frontier and pioneer life — West (U.S.) — Maps for children. [1. United States — Territorial expansion — Maps. 2. West (U.S.) — History — Maps. 3. Frontier and pioneer life — west (U.S) — Maps. 4. Atlases.]
I. Title. II. Series.

E179.5.F385 2004
911'.73 — dc22

                                                                                    2003070402

Manufactured in the United States of America

On the cover: Top: A portrait of President Andrew Jackson (1767–1837), who served a term from 1829 to 1837. Bottom: Immigrants of North America crossing the plains in covered wagons. Background: A map of the United States from the Mississippi River to the Pacific Ocean.

Contents

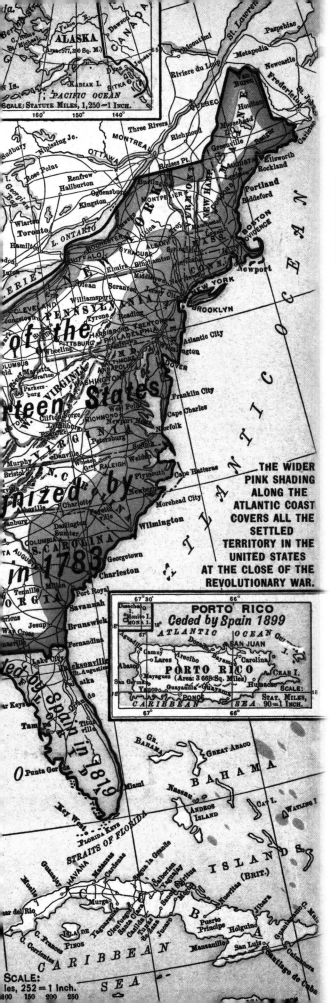

THE WIDER PINK SHADING ALONG THE ATLANTIC COAST COVERS ALL THE SETTLED TERRITORY IN THE UNITED STATES AT THE CLOSE OF THE REVOLUTIONARY WAR.

INTRODUCTION

For the United States, the nineteenth century was a time of rapid population growth and land expansion. According to U.S. census figures, the population was 5,309,000 in 1800. Within a century, by 1900, it had exploded to 75,995,000 people. (These numbers do not include untaxed Native Americans.) Immigration and high birth rates helped the population soar.

The nation's land size also grew as the country expanded westward. The Louisiana Purchase in 1803 doubled the nation's size. In 1845, Texas was annexed. Then in 1846, the United States obtained the Oregon Territory from Great Britain. After the Mexican-American War (1846–1848), New Mexico and California became U.S. territories.

This map of the United States illustrates the original states in 1783, from the Atlantic coast to the Mississippi River. Other territories that became part of the country from 1783 through the 1850s are also represented, but designated by different colors. During the nineteenth century, American settlers moved farther and farther west in search of adequate farmland and new opportunities. For the Native Americans who had lived on the land for centuries, this migration meant a loss of land and livelihood.

The angel Columbia in this 1872 lithograph by George A. Crofutt is symbolic of the yearning by Americans to move west during the nineteenth century. Most Americans believed it was their God-given right to capture a piece of the developing nation, an idea known as manifest destiny. Pioneers gathered in Missouri every spring and then traveled together for safety in wagon trains heading west across the Great Plains in search of new land and new lives.

By 1875, the nation had expanded west as far as the Pacific Ocean. In addition, it had purchased the Alaska Territory from Russia in 1867.

Much of the West was already home to Native American tribes who had lived on the land long before the arrival of Europeans. But

in the spirit of manifest destiny, Americans took more and more land from the Indians. They explored these territories and settled them. Church missionaries taught Protestant beliefs to Indian tribes.

Manifest destiny was a way of looking at politics and religion. In the spirit of manifest destiny, Americans believed their duty was to expand across the continent from ocean to ocean. They intended to settle the land, establish a democratic government, and teach Protestant religious beliefs.

John O'Sullivan coined the term "manifest destiny" in 1845. That summer, Americans were debating whether to annex Texas. O'Sullivan wrote an editorial in favor of the annexation for the *United States Magazine and Democratic Review*. He wrote about "our manifest destiny to overspread the continent allotted by Providence." This land was destined "for the free development of our yearly multiplying millions." In other words, it was God's plan for the United States to expand westward.

By 1875, Americans controlled territory from the Atlantic Ocean to the Pacific Ocean. Very little land remained for exploration. Due to westward expansion, the frontier had been conquered and settled.

CHAPTER ONE
Claiming the West

In the 1780s, the United States lay along North America's eastern edge. Originally, the thirteen colonies had stretched from the Atlantic Ocean to the Appalachian Mountains. Then, in 1783, Great Britain gave more land to the United States, and the country's territory expanded from the Appalachian Mountains to the Mississippi River. At the time, much of this frontier territory and land to its west remained a mystery to colonists. But soon, explorers and trappers would open up this land to Americans. In part, this expansion was due to the actions of Thomas Jefferson, the third president of the United States. Jefferson added new territory to the nation and sent explorers to survey it.

The presidential election of 1800 was intense. The two major candidates were

The original thirteen states are seen in this detail of a United States map from 1783. Within twenty years of the initial land acquisition from Great Britain in 1783, President Thomas Jefferson doubled the size of the United States. He organized an agreement with France's Napoléon to buy the Louisiana Territory for $15 million (see the Province of Louisiana on map, page 4) in 1803. After the deal was settled, Jefferson sent groups of men to explore the land and its inhabitants. The most famous of these groups was the Corps of Discovery.

The Thirteen Colonies
Other British Colonies
Crown lands reserved for Indians by proclamation of 1763, and claimed by colonies lying to the eastward
_____ _Proclamation Line of 1763_
•—•—• _Boone's Trail, 1769_ o—o—o _Robertson's Trail, 1774_
TRANSYLVANIA: _Proposed western colonies_
✦ Fort, CONN.= _Connecticut;_ DEL.C.= _Delaware Counties_
✕ _Battle_ **Spanish possessions**
French

For the approximate location of Indian tribes in the western country, see page 188, and for the vicinity of the WATAUGA ASSOCIATION, _see page 196._

Scale 1 : 20 000 000

Miles.

Scale 1 : 10 000 000

Miles.

Jefferson and John Adams. Adams had been elected president in 1796. As a Federalist, he wanted a strong national government. His opponent, Jefferson, was also his vice president. Jefferson, a Democratic-Republican, favored strong states' rights. In the press, supporters of one candidate exaggerated the other candidate's weaknesses. Jefferson even paid some journalists to libel Adams. Libel is the publication of unfavorable comments about someone unjustly. Jefferson, the author of the Declaration of Independence, won the election. During his term in office, he made an important decision to claim new land for Americans.

Westward Expansion

President Jefferson took office in 1801. Within the first two years of his administration, the nation's size had almost doubled. This expansion happened nearly by accident. Americans needed to use the New Orleans port to dock their ships, but it was located in the Louisiana Territory, which was owned by France. The Louisiana Territory stretched from the Mississippi River to the Rocky Mountains and included some of present-day Texas and Louisiana. In order to gain this land, Jefferson sent Robert Livingston to negotiate with the emperor of France, Napoléon Bonaparte.

At this time, France was at war with Great Britain. In order to continue fighting the British, Napoléon needed money. To generate funds, France offered to sell the Louisiana Territory to the United States in order to support its war effort. In 1803, Jefferson and Congress approved the Louisiana Purchase from France at a cost of $15 million. In return, the United States gained more than 800,000 square miles (2,071,990 square kilometers) of unexplored land.

Thomas Jefferson (1743–1826) served the United States as its third president from 1801 to 1809. Despite his abilities as an eloquent writer who drafted the Declaration of Independence, Jefferson was an awkward public speaker.

American artist Charles Willson Peale painted these portraits of Meriwether Lewis *(left)* and William Clark *(right)* in 1807. Lewis, who at the time was serving as secretary to President Jefferson, asked Clark to join the Corps of Discovery, an expedition party that headed west from 1804 to 1806. Lewis and Clark, friends for years after once serving together in the U.S. Army, made detailed observations of their journey. Together they mapped trails, noted flora and fauna, and communicated with Native Americans.

Jefferson wanted U.S. citizens to survey the new territory in order to find a water route across it to the Pacific Ocean. He asked Meriwether Lewis and William Clark to find this Northwest Passage. Lewis and Clark formed the Corps of Discovery, an expedition that included soldiers, outdoorsmen, and a slave. Along the way, they took on interpreters who spoke the various languages of the Indians who lived on the land. One of the interpreters was Sacagawea, a Shoshone Indian woman.

In May 1804, Lewis and Clark set out from St. Louis, Missouri, and traveled up the Missouri River. Clark carefully mapped each bend of the waterway. Lewis greeted the Native Americans he met and learned about their culture. By winter, the Corps of Discovery had reached present-day North Dakota. In the spring, they sent maps back home. Then the corps pushed farther west. They found the mouth of the Missouri River and traveled down the Clearwater, Snake, and Columbia Rivers. At last, in November 1805,

Discove

Cape Disappointment
Fort Clatsop National Memorial
Ridgefield National Wildlife Refuge
Columbia River Gorge National Scenic Area

National Historic Landmark
Lolo Trail
Lewis and Clark
National Historic Trail
Interpretive Center
Upper Missouri River Breaks
National Monument

Station
Camp
National Historical Park
Nez Perce
SPOKANE

WASHINGTON
SEATTLE

Rock
Fort
PORTLAND
RICHLAND

Tamastslikt
Cultural Institute

OREGON

IDAHO

Lewis and Clark
Pass

Travelers' Rest
State Park

Gibbons
Pass

Lost Trail
Pass

Lemhi Pass
National Historic Landmark

Camp Fortunate

Beaverhead Rock

Three Forks

Gates of the Mountains

MONTANA

Charles M. Russell
National Wildlife Refuge

GREAT
FALLS

Pompeys Pillar
National Monument

BILLINGS

Northern Cheyenne

Confluence of Yellowstone and
Missouri Rivers

Three Tribes Museum

Fort Berthold Rese
Knife River
Indian Villages
National Historic Site

Fort Manda
Interpretive

BISMARCK

On-a-Slant Indian Village

NORTH DAKO

Standing Rock IR

Cheyenne River IR

SOU

Bad River
Confluence

PIERRE

Th

WYOMING

Wind River
Indian Reservation

Missouri National Recr

Louisiana

Lewis

Fort Atkinso
NEBRA

NEVADA

SALT LAKE CITY

UTAH

CHEYENNE

DENVER

COLORADO

Purchas

KAN

CALIFORNIA

SAN FRANCISCO

SACRAMENTO

Arkansas
River

LAS
VEGAS

LOS ANGELES

ARIZONA

Navajo Indian Reservation

Southern Ute
Jicarilla Apache

Taos R.

ALBUQUERQUE

NEW MEXICO

WICHITA FALLS

LUBBOCK

SAN DIEGO

PHOENIX

Fort Apache IR

San Carlos IR

Tohono O'odham
IR

San Xavier IR

Mescalero Apache IR

EL PASO

TEXAS

SAN ANTONIO

ATLANTIC
OCEAN

FORT CLATSOP

ST. LOUIS
MONTICELLO

PACIFIC OCEAN

Preparation

Recruitment

Exploration and
Homecoming

Indian Reservation

Louisiana Purchase
Boundary

Lewis and Clark
National Historic Trail

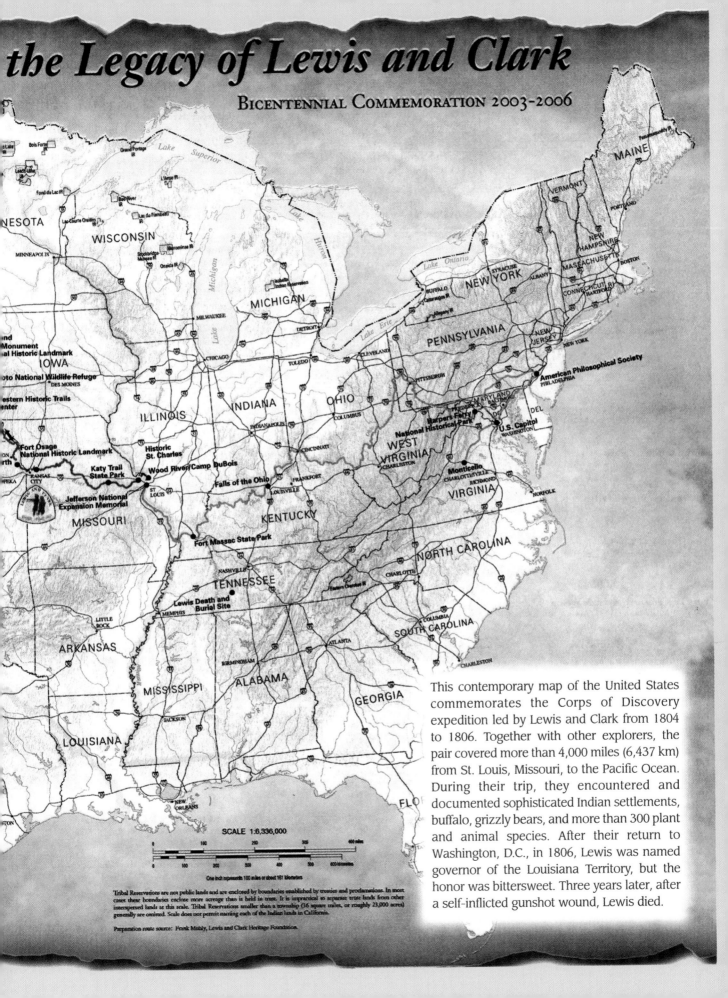

the Legacy of Lewis and Clark

Bicentennial Commemoration 2003–2006

This contemporary map of the United States commemorates the Corps of Discovery expedition led by Lewis and Clark from 1804 to 1806. Together with other explorers, the pair covered more than 4,000 miles (6,437 km) from St. Louis, Missouri, to the Pacific Ocean. During their trip, they encountered and documented sophisticated Indian settlements, buffalo, grizzly bears, and more than 300 plant and animal species. After their return to Washington, D.C., in 1806, Lewis was named governor of the Louisiana Territory, but the honor was bittersweet. Three years later, after a self-inflicted gunshot wound, Lewis died.

SCALE 1:6,336,000

One inch represents 100 miles or about 161 kilometers

Tribal Reservations are not public lands and are enclosed by boundaries established by treaties and proclamations. In most cases these boundaries enclose more acreage than is held in trust. It is impractical to separate trust lands from other interspersed lands at this scale. Tribal Reservations smaller than a township (36 square miles, or roughly 23,000 acres) generally are omitted. Scale does not permit naming each of the Indian lands in California.

Preparation route source: Frank Muhly, Lewis and Clark Heritage Foundation.

they reached the Pacific Coast. The journey had taken a year and a half. Along the way, Lewis and Clark kept many diaries. Their writings described the geography, plants, animals, and native peoples of the Louisiana Territory and land to its west. This information, along with their accurate maps, helped open the West to pioneers.

The Lewis and Clark expedition also inspired trappers like Jim Bridger, Jedediah Smith, and James Beckwourth. These "mountain men" hiked deep into the forests and mountains, where they trapped beavers

Pikes Peak

Pikes Peak in Colorado is named after the American explorer and military officer Zebulon Montgomery Pike. In 1806, Lieutenant Pike led fifteen explorers into the southern Louisiana Territory. At one point, Pike saw and tried to climb an extremely tall mountain, which later became known as Pikes Peak.

Pike also tried to find the headwaters of the Arkansas River and the Red River, but failed. However, his journey was valuable for other reasons. He made contact with and documented the activities of many Native American tribes. His reports inspired traders to travel to the Southwest.

The view from atop Pikes Peak is so breathtaking that it was the inspiration for the lyrics to the song "America the Beautiful," written by author and teacher Katharine Lee Bates in 1893. Today, visitors can reach the summit of Pikes Peak—some 7,500 feet (2,286 m) in the air—by railway on the Pikes Peak Cog Railroad or by car on the Pikes Peak Toll Road.

and other fur-bearing animals. Many trappers worked for fur companies such as John Jacob Astor's American Fur Company and the Rocky Mountain Fur Company. These trappers also helped map the American frontier.

Bridger was the first white man to see the Great Salt Lake. Smith found South Pass in the Rocky Mountains in present-day Wyoming. Later, settlers would use South Pass on the Oregon Trail. Beckwourth, an African American, found Beckwourth Pass in California's Sierra Nevada.

Battles over Land

The United States won its independence from Great Britain in the Revolutionary War, which ended in 1783. However, conflict still brewed between both nations. On June 18, 1812, the United States declared war on Great Britain. Known as the War of 1812, it mostly involved disputes over land claims in North America.

Both the United States and Great Britain claimed land near Canada, then known as British North America. Great Britain continued to build forts in the Northwest Territory, and the British stirred up conflicts between Native Americans and U.S. pioneers, making it more difficult for American frontiersman to settle the land. The British were also weakening the American economy by interfering with American shipping to France.

The United States was poorly equipped to fight another war and had only six warships and a small army of 6,700 men. When Americans invaded British territory in Canada, they were beaten. Indians took advantage of this defeat by attacking American settlers. The Indians wanted to drive the pioneers from Indian land. One of the most influential Indian leaders was Tecumseh, a Shawnee chief. He and his brother, the Prophet, convinced other tribes to support the British.

As a result, Americans had to fight Indian warriors and British soldiers. Battles raged over control of Lake Erie, Lake Ontario, Lake Champlain, and Lake Michigan. By 1814, the British controlled Lake Michigan. They also controlled the northern Mississippi River and invaded Chesapeake Bay. The British burned buildings in Washington, D.C., and set fire to the White House.

By the end of 1814, the United States and Great Britain had reached their limits. Neither country was winning the war, and both had exhausted their resources. They signed the Treaty of Ghent on December 24, 1814, which ended the war and set the border between the United States and Canada.

This map depicts areas of fighting on land between the United States and Great Britain during the War of 1812. Unfair trade practices by the British, including search and seizure operations on the high seas and the impressment (forced service) of American sailors into British service, were among the conflicts that led the United States to war. In 1814, both countries called off their troops and signed the Treaty of Ghent.

Under the treaty, both the United States and Great Britain would control the Oregon Territory. Both countries had fought for this northwestern territory because it was a valuable resource for the profitable fur trade.

News of the treaty did not immediately reach the southern United States. In January 1815, U.S. soldiers defeated British troops at the Battle of New Orleans. The hero of this battle was General Andrew Jackson, often called by his nickname,

"Old Hickory." Jackson would become president of the United States in 1829.

Neither the British nor the Americans won the War of 1812. However, Americans liked to feel they were victorious anyway. This feeling was due to winning the Battle of New Orleans. It was also due to the death of Tecumseh. A feeling of nationalism grew in U.S. citizens because they had withstood the pressure of Great Britain, then the strongest empire of the world.

After the War of 1812, U.S. leaders made a decision to halt the further development of European colonies. Americans wanted all the land for themselves. In 1823, President James Monroe spoke to Congress and said the Western Hemisphere was closed to colonization. His speech, called the "Monroe Doctrine," marked the end of European domination in the Americas.

Transportation and Maps

In the early days, travel was slow due to rough landscapes and few developed roads. Transportation by waterway was sometimes possible, but rivers did not go everywhere people needed to travel. In addition, navigating in new territories was difficult and dangerous. The land was poorly

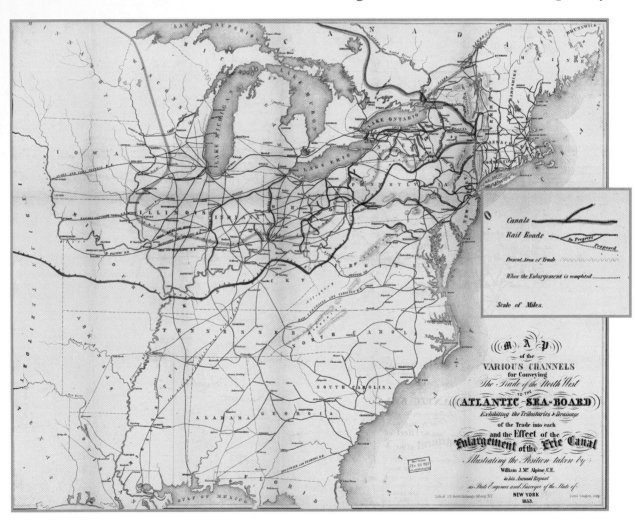

This map of the eastern half of the United States illustrates canals, finished railroads, and railroads in progress during the time of the map's creation in 1853. The Erie Canal, which connected the Great Lakes with New York City via the Hudson River beginning in 1825, helped speed the growth and development of the upper Midwest. Transportation along the canal helped provide New York City with a continuous supply of fresh fruits and vegetables.

mapped, and inexperienced travelers often became lost or injured.

Canals, or man-made waterways, helped solve the travel problem. One of the most important was the Erie Canal, which was built by Irish immigrants between 1817 and 1825. It linked Albany, New York, and the Hudson River in the east, and Buffalo (along the U.S.-Canada border) and the Great Lakes in the west. The Erie Canal was 363 miles (584 km) long and 40 feet (12 m) wide. After it was finished, a journey that once took weeks to complete now took only days. New York Harbor quickly became the nation's most valuable shipping port. Because of its success, more than 4,000 miles (6,437 km) of canals were in use by 1840.

Accurate maps were also important to travelers throughout the new territory. In 1838, the U.S. Army formed the Corps of Topographical Engineers, whose members were primarily mapmakers. Bit by bit, they surveyed the frontier during the 1840s to the 1860s.

The corps found the best routes into the frontier for settlers. One well-known engineer, John Charles Frémont, made the frontier sound romantic, even magical. He described it with excitement, and his reporting inspired many people to go west. Explorers such as Lewis and Clark and Frémont stirred Americans' curiosity. People risked their lives to claim their own land. Others traveled west for gold, which was discovered in California in 1848.

Population Growth

Population boomed during the early 1800s. In 1800, the U.S. population was about 5 million, but with high birth rates and steady immigration, it kept growing. By 1830, the Ohio Valley was home to nearly 1 million settlers. By the middle of the century, the U.S. population was around 23 million.

These people needed somewhere to live, but the frontier was still home to many Native Americans. Most settlers believed the land belonged to the United States. They felt that they had a right to move west. Americans believed it was their duty to "civilize" the Indians. They forced Indians to adopt white culture and religion. In the spirit of manifest destiny, settlers poured into the frontier and pushed the Indians westward.

CHAPTER TWO
Pushing Westward

Early contact between colonists and Native Americans was friendly. The Indians showed settlers how to grow beans, corn, squash, and tobacco. They introduced settlers to the fun of sledding on the snow and showed them how to make snowshoes and canoes.

But more settlers pushed into Indian lands. They began claiming the land for themselves and pushed the Indians farther west. The settlers built fences, chopped down trees, and slaughtered herds of buffalo. These changes made it difficult for tribes to live as they always had. They moved west in search of unsettled land. Eventually, whites used warfare to force the Indians off their land.

Indian Removal

The official policy of removing Native Americans from their land began after the War of 1812. In part, the United States was punishing some Indians for supporting the British. American leaders made Indian leaders sign treaties, which opened huge chunks of land to whites. For example, between 1817 and 1821, several dozen tribes in the Ohio Valley were forced on to reservations. Those who refused to migrate had to move farther into the wilderness. This area later became Illinois, Indiana, and Michigan.

General Andrew Jackson, seen in this lithograph in 1814, eventually became the seventh president of the United States, serving from 1829 to 1837. Jackson served as a general in the War of 1812 and defeated the British during the Battle of New Orleans.

up 23 million acres (9.3 million hectares) of land. Unfortunately, this land also belonged to the White Sticks who had helped Jackson.

After the War of 1812, Jackson continually led armies of frontiersmen against Indians. He forced many tribes to sign treaties and took their land. These areas became Florida, Georgia, Mississippi, North Carolina, and Kentucky. In 1829, Jackson was elected president of the United States. Early in his term, he helped pass the Indian Removal Act (1830). This act was meant to remove Native Americans from their land and relocate them to Indian Territory in Oklahoma.

The Cherokee Indians fought back and took their case to the U.S. Supreme Court. They claimed it

A leader in Indian removal was Andrew Jackson. He fought against Indians during the War of 1812. One conflict was with the Creek Indians. Their land totaled more than 40 million acres (16 million hectares). In 1813, Jackson's troops battled Creeks (the Red Sticks). He got other Creeks (the White Sticks) to help him. The next year, Jackson's forces won the Battle of Horseshoe Bend. He insisted the Creeks sign a treaty that forced them to give

In this illustration, General Andrew Jackson and the Tennessee militia defeated the Creek Indians in one of the last battles during the War of 1812. The Creeks were forced to sign a peace treaty with the U.S. government that opened their lands to American expansionism.

Routes of Cherokee Removal

— Land route
— Water route
— Other major routes

Illinois

Missouri

Kansas

Kentucky

Cape Giradeau
Springfield

Hopkinsville

Tennessee

Fayetteville

Nashville

Charleston

Evansville

Arkansas

Memphis

Chattanooga

Fort Smith

Mississippi River

Tahlequah
Little Rock

Fort Payne

New Echota

Oklahoma

Mississippi

Alabama

Georgia

The Cherokee Indians had been pushed out of their indigenous lands since the time of the American Revolution, but it wasn't until the 1800s that they were completely forced off their remaining settlements. This migration is known as the Trail of Tears. More than 4,000 Cherokee died during the forced march, which took place during the winter of 1838 to 1839. The United States government considered the act of forcing Indians off their lands legal under the Indian Removal Act of 1830.

Manifest Destiny and Racism

In the 1800s, many Americans spoke of manifest destiny. This mission was to conquer and settle the country from "ocean to shining ocean." But manifest destiny was not just about land. It was about race, too. Many Americans believed the white race was superior to any others. They thought Asians, blacks, Native Americans, and Mexicans were inferior. To whites, the languages, religions, and living styles of other races were inferior.

Many whites tried to change other races. They wanted to make them more like whites. What they could not change, they conquered. Missionaries worked to convert Native Americans to "white" religions. Political leaders like Andrew Jackson forced Native Americans to give up their lands. In some states, whites forced blacks to work as slaves. Other states segregated (separated) whites from blacks. These are just a few examples of the racism that was part of manifest destiny.

was illegal for the United States to take their land. The Supreme Court agreed with the Cherokee. Despite that decision, President Jackson forced the Cherokee to move to the Indian Territory. To get there, they had to walk 1,200 miles (1,931 km). One third of the 14,000 Cherokee died during the journey, mostly due to starvation or illness. That forced march is known as the Trail of Tears.

Native American Resistance

Being forced off their lands was a terrible experience for Native Americans, and many fought back. They terrorized settlers who moved onto their land. They raided wagon trains and fought U.S. Army troops.

One of the most famous Native American heroes was Tecumseh.

Just before the War of 1812, Tecumseh's brother, the Prophet, clashed with General William Henry Harrison. They fought on the banks of the Tippecanoe River where the Prophet's warriors were beaten. This defeat inspired Tecumseh to fight even harder.

On October 5, 1813, Tecumseh joined the British in a battle with American soldiers. The groups clashed on the banks of the Thames River, in what is now Ontario, Canada. Then British troops pulled back. However, Tecumseh and his warriors continued fighting, and Tecumseh died.

Farther to the south, another group of Indians resisted America's manifest destiny. They were the Seminole Indians of Florida. In the beginning, Florida was under

The Shawnee Indian chief Tecumseh, who was likely killed by William Henry Harrison, is pictured in this illustration that shows both men in battle on the Thames River. Tecumseh had joined forces with the British to make it more difficult for the Americans to take Indian lands. At the time, Harrison was governor of the Indiana Territory. He had disrupted Indian villages in what later became Indiana and Illinois in order to gain control of more land.

Spanish control, but even Spain could not keep General Andrew Jackson away. In the First Seminole War (1817–1818) Jackson led forces against Seminole tribes. One reason for his attacks was to recapture runaway slaves. Many escaped slaves were living among Seminole tribes. Jackson's military campaign attacked both the Seminoles and Spanish settlements. His soldiers burned Spanish villages and razed Spanish forts. Jackson's actions helped push Spain to sell Florida to the United States for 5 million dollars in 1819. Jackson then became governor of the Florida Territory.

In this painting by John F. Clymer, American forces travel by boat through the Florida swamplands while Seminole Indians hide behind cypress trees on the shore. The Seminole Wars were a series of conflicts between Americans and Seminole Indians between 1817 and 1858. Ultimately, the Seminole Indians were completely forced off their lands, and the United States gained control of Florida.

The Second Seminole War was fought between 1835 and 1842. This time, U.S. forces tried to move the Seminoles west. They wanted their land and used the Indian Removal Act to get it. The Seminoles, led by Chief Osceola, resisted and hid in the Everglades. They fought back using unusual tactics such as sabotage and harassment. This war was bloody and expensive for the United States. It finally ended with the capture of Chief Osceola. After this, most Seminoles moved west, across the Mississippi River. The few who remained in Florida settled on distant swamplands. In the Third Seminole War (1855–1858), U.S. troops forced the last Seminole tribes west.

CHAPTER THREE
New Territories

The United States was still growing rapidly during the 1850s. At that time, U.S. territory stretched to the Rocky Mountains in the northwest and to Spanish territory in the south.

This growth finally stopped because of the northern boundary with Canada and the southern boundary with Mexico. But Americans did not accept boundaries easily. In the early 1800s, they fought Great Britain over the placement of the Canadian border. Later, during the Mexican-American War, Americans fought over southern boundaries. These wars and other U.S. land purchases expanded U.S. territory.

Gradually, territories were divided into separate states. Between 1800 and 1850, fifteen new states joined the nation, and by 1875, six additional states were formed, creating a total of thirty-seven.

This map illustrates the growth of the United States and the relationships between states and territories between 1783 and 1912. The United States expanded as a result of negotiated settlements, forced annexations, and financial agreements. As the population of each new colonized area grew, it became eligible for admission into the Union as a fully fledged state with its own laws.

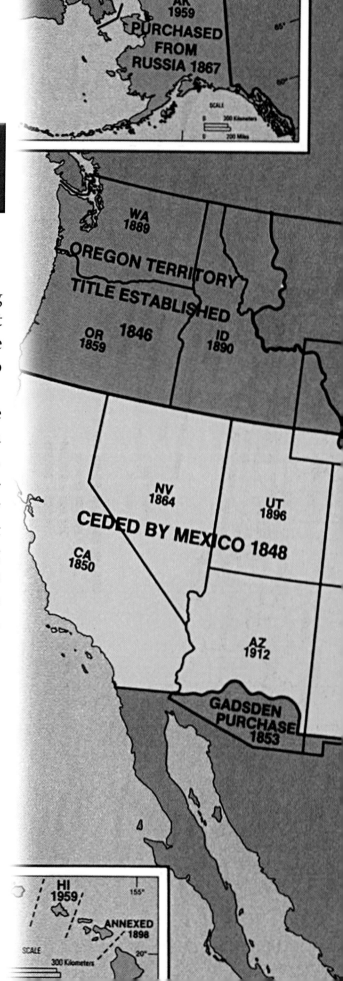

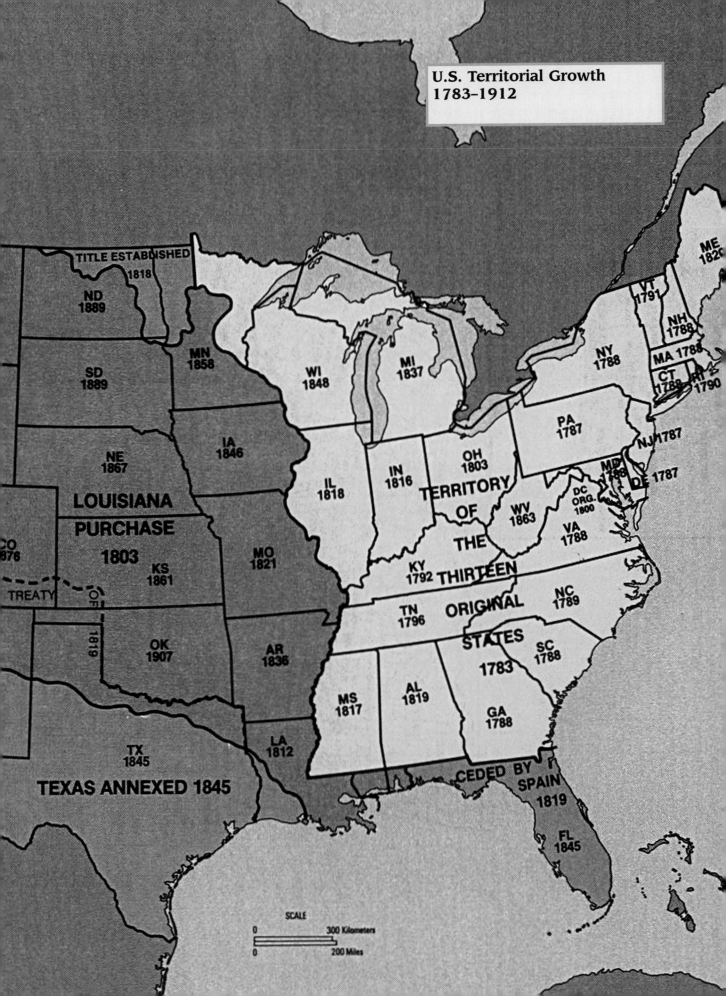

U.S. Territorial Growth
1783–1912

TITLE ESTABLISHED 1818

ND
1889

SD
1889

MN
1858

ME
1820

VT
1791

NH
1788

NY
1788

MA 1788

CT
1788

RI
1790

WI
1848

MI
1837

PA
1787

NJ 1787

NE
1867

IA
1846

OH
1803

MD
1788

DE 1787

LOUISIANA

PURCHASE

1803

CO
1876

IL
1818

IN
1816

TERRITORY

OF

WV
1863

DC
ORG.
1800

VA
1788

KS
1861

MO
1821

THE

KY
1792

THIRTEEN

TREATY

OF

1819

TN
1796

ORIGINAL

NC
1789

OK
1907

AR
1836

STATES

SC
1788

1783

AL
1819

MS
1817

GA
1788

TX
1845

LA
1812

TEXAS ANNEXED 1845

CEDED BY SPAIN
1819

FL
1845

SCALE

0   300 Kilometers

0   200 Miles

Texas and Mexico

"Remember the Alamo!" Many Americans, especially Texans, are familiar with this battle cry. It represents a time of conflict with Mexico. During this time, Texas broke apart from Mexico in the 1830s and formed the Republic of Texas, an independent nation.

Texas was first a homeland to Native Americans. Beginning in the 1500s, Spain explored and claimed land in the New World. By 1800, Spain controlled present-day Mexico and the regions of California, New Mexico, and Texas. Then, in 1821, the Republic of Mexico won independence from Spain. Afterward, Mexico controlled all this land.

To attract settlers, Mexico set up the empresario system. Under this agreement, settlers received free land in Mexico's northern region. One person was granted enough ranch land and farmland for 100 families. The new owner was in charge of bringing in settlers. In return, settlers agreed to worship as Roman Catholics. After the empresario system was established, the first to come were the "old three hundred."

This woodcut depicts the death of Davy Crockett at the fall of the Alamo during the Texas War of Independence in 1836. While some 180 Texans died defending the Republic of Texas from Mexican forces, Texas military commander Sam Houston had enough time to mount a counterattack against Mexican troops.

Stephen F. Austin moved these 300 families to Texas beginning in 1821.

Americans poured into Mexican territory, but most did not convert to Catholicism as they had promised. They continued to worship as Protestants. Nor did they become Mexican citizens. In fact, they had little respect for the distant Mexican government. Americans soon out-numbered Mexicans. In 1830, Mexico ordered American settlers to stop coming. Although Mexican troops marched into Texas to restore Mexican control over the area, U.S. citizens kept arriving.

In 1836, Texans formed the Republic of Texas. Although they won some early battles with Mexican troops, General Antonio López de Santa Anna, the president of Mexico, attacked Texans at the Alamo on February 23, 1836. Some famous Americans such as Davy Crockett and James Bowie helped defend the old mission-fort. Their leader was Lieutenant Colonel William B. Travis. The battle lasted twelve days, and 1,600 Mexicans and at least 180 Texans died. In the end, Santa Anna was victorious.

Soon after, the Texas military commander, Sam Houston, attack-ed Santa Anna on the banks of the San Jacinto River. In just a few min-utes, while shouting, "Remember the Alamo!," Houston defeated Santa Anna on April 25, 1836. About three weeks later, on May 14, Texas signed a treaty with Santa Anna that set boundaries for the Republic of Texas. Today Texas's southern land border remains the Rio Grande River.

Although Texas wanted to become part of the United States, the process was slow. A big obstacle was the issue of slavery. Northern states that opposed slavery did not want another state that allowed slavery in the Union. However, Southern states wanted Texas to remain a slave state. Because of this disagreement, President Andrew Jackson decided not to annex Texas. In his opinion, the balance of peace between states was too fragile.

Nine years later, in 1845, James K. Polk was president. He and the previous president, John Tyler, wit-nessed Mexican troops and Indians invading and raiding Texas's settle-ments. Texas needed military help, so in 1846, the United States annexed Texas and it became the twenty-eighth state.

The Texas annexation led to war with Mexico. For one thing, Mexico rejected the treaty Santa Anna had signed, claiming Texas was still a Mexican possession. Also, the United States and Mexico disagreed over Texas's southern boundary. American troops entered the disputed land between the Nueces and the Rio Grande Rivers. Mexican troops marched north to the Rio Grande, where fighting broke out in April 1846. Soon after, President Polk declared war on Mexico.

Fighting went on for more than a year. The United States won victory after victory, and American troops occupied California and New Mexico. On September 14, 1847, General Winfield Scott captured Mexico City, the Mexican capital. After this defeat, the fighting stopped.

The Mexican-American War ended in 1848, and both sides signed the Treaty of Guadalupe Hidalgo. Under the treaty, Mexico ceded more land to the United States for $15 million. Today, this land is sections of California, Utah, Nevada, Arizona, New Mexico, Texas, and western Colorado.

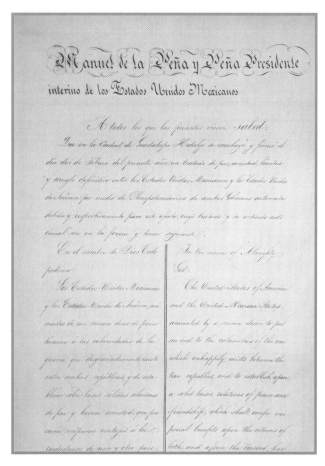

The Treaty of Guadalupe Hidalgo, shown here, was an agreement signed between the United States and Mexico in 1848 that ended the Mexican-American War. According to its provisions, Mexico ceded 55 percent of its territory in exchange for $15 million. This territory included sections of what are now Arizona, California, New Mexico, Texas, Colorado, Nevada, and Utah. The treaty set the U.S.–Mexico boundary line at the Rio Grande.

The Oregon Territory

The Oregon Territory was an area in the distant northwest. Today, this land forms Oregon, Washington, Idaho, and part of Montana. In the early 1800s, Great Britain and the United States shared control of the Oregon Territory. Lewis and Clark traveled through the region in 1805. During the 1830s, American missionaries moved there, and by the 1840s, many Americans wanted the Oregon Territory to become a U.S. possession.

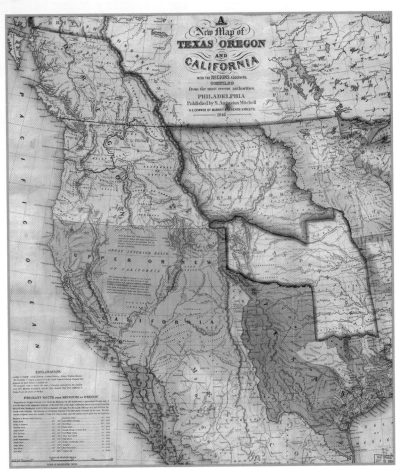

This map of the western United States was created after Great Britain signed the Oregon Treaty, allowing Americans authority over the Oregon Territory. Americans demanded control of the expansive territory beginning in 1844, but problems with the Mexican-American War forced a delay of the final agreement until 1846, the same year this map was created.

Some Americans were willing to fight for Oregon, but there was to be no war. The U.S. secretary of state, James Buchanan, opened talks with Great Britain. After much discussion, the two countries signed the Oregon Treaty on June 18, 1846. The treaty declared Oregon to be a U.S. territory. It set the forty-ninth parallel as the boundary between Oregon and Canada.

Then in 1853, the United States finalized its southern boundary with Mexico. It did so with the Gadsden Purchase. For $10 million, the United States bought about 29,000 square miles (75,100 sq km). This land lay along the southern edge of the New Mexico Territory. This purchase was an important point in U.S. history: it represented the final addition to the land that forms the forty-eight contiguous (adjacent) states. (Alaska and Hawaii later became U.S. states in 1959.)

CHAPTER FOUR
Blazing Trails

More than 150,000 immigrants settled in the United States between 1820 and 1830. During the next decade, 600,000 arrived. By 1860, more than 4 million more immigrants had made the United States their home. By 1875, the U.S. population was nearly 45 million.

Immigrants and native-born Americans built new towns and swelled existing cities before the West opened up as a frontier. First, explorers blazed trails across the Great Plains and the Rocky Mountains, and then families headed west.

Trails West

The first route heading west was the Santa Fe Trail. It linked Franklin, Missouri, to Santa Fe in the Mexican territory. For American traders, the Santa Fe Trail became an important route to Mexican markets.

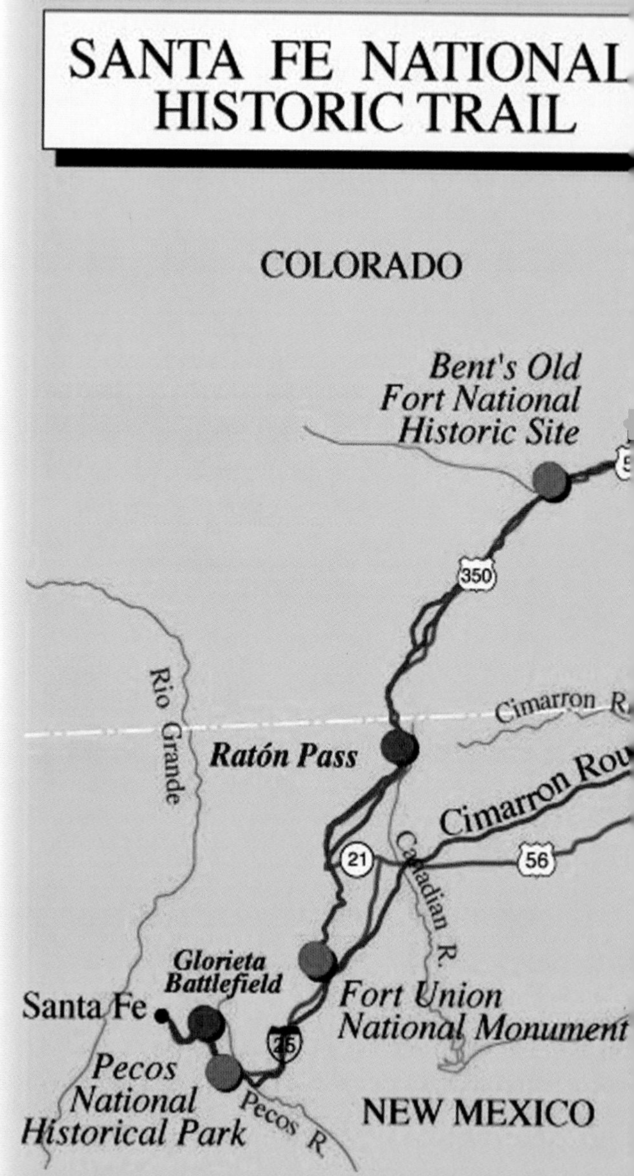

The historic Santa Fe Trail was an important U.S. trade route for the transport of silver and fur, and later, manufactured goods. In the 1820s, William Becknell, a trader who traveled the route between what is now Independence, Missouri, to Santa Fe, New Mexico, blazed the original trail.

SANTA FE NATIONAL HISTORIC TRAIL

COLORADO

Bent's Old Fort National Historic Site

Rio Grande

Ratón Pass

Cimarron R.

Cimarron Route

Glorieta Battlefield

Santa Fe

Pecos National Historical Park

Pecos R.

Canadian R.

Fort Union National Monument

NEW MEXICO

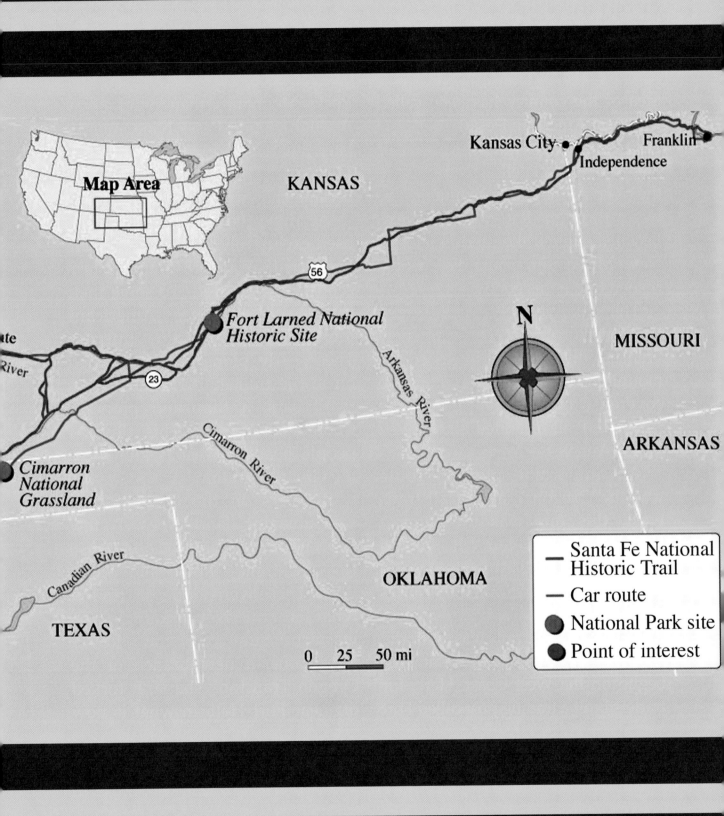

Map Area

KANSAS

Kansas City

Franklin

Independence

56

Fort Larned National
Historic Site

Arkansas River

N

MISSOURI

ute

River

23

Cimarron River

ARKANSAS

Cimarron
National
Grassland

Canadian River

OKLAHOMA

TEXAS

0   25   50 mi

Santa Fe National
Historic Trail

Car route

National Park site

Point of interest

William Becknell, a trader, blazed the Santa Fe Trail. In 1821, he took his mule train through the grassy plains that are now present-day Kansas and reached the Arkansas River. This area of the country has been called the Great American Desert. Its rolling prairies seemed endless, and water was scarce. Becknell stayed close to the river. At the Rocky Mountains, he went through Raton Pass. Next, Becknell entered the sandy plains of New Mexico. In Santa Fe, people rushed to buy his goods.

The next year, Becknell blazed the Cimarron Cutoff. This was a new branch of the trail that bypassed the mountains and was better suited to covered-wagon travel. Later, the Santa Fe Trail extended all the way to Los Angeles.

An important pioneer route was the Oregon Trail. Of all trails west, this one was the longest and most traveled. It linked Independence, Missouri, to Astoria in the Oregon Territory, 2,000 miles (3,200 km) away.

The Oregon Trail was actually blazed in reverse. That is, it was begun on the West Coast. Here, fur traders built a trading post called Fort Astoria in 1811. During an attack by Indians, their ship was destroyed, and they were stranded. In June 1812, a small group led by Robert Stuart, a partner in the Pacific Fur Company, went for help by following rivers east. Along the way, Crow Indians stole their horses, but Shoshone Indians showed them a better route. In the Rocky Mountains, they found a way through South Pass. Nine months later, Stuart's group reached St. Louis, Missouri. Their route eventually became known as the Oregon Trail.

At first, the Oregon Trail was used exclusively by trappers. Then, between 1837 and 1842, the eastern economy weakened. To solve their financial problems, Americans looked west with new interest. These early pioneers first trickled on to the trail in 1841, and within two years, a thousand pioneers flooded the route. This flow of people heading west is known as the Great Migration.

Pioneers on the Oregon Trail saw amazing landscapes. A few key features were Courthouse Rock, Chimney Rock, and Scotts Bluff. These were along the trail in what is now Nebraska. On the western side of the Rocky Mountains, a new branch of the Oregon Trail took shape. It forked off near Fort Hall, in what is now Utah. This section, the California Trail, led to California. In 1849, it became important during the California gold rush.

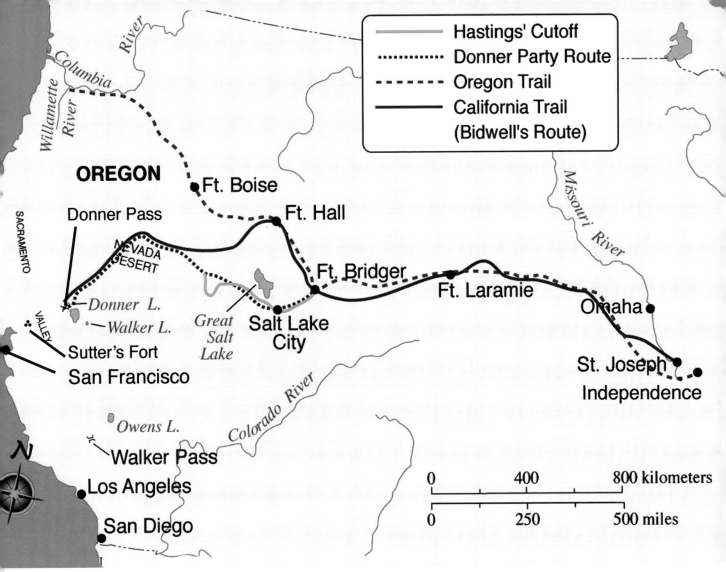

OREGON

Donner Pass

Ft. Boise

Ft. Hall

NEVADA DESERT

Donner L.

Walker L.

Great Salt Lake

Salt Lake City

Ft. Bridger

Ft. Laramie

Omaha

Sutter's Fort

San Francisco

St. Joseph

Independence

Owens L.

Walker Pass

Los Angeles

San Diego

Columbia River

Willamette River

SACRAMENTO

VALLEY

Colorado River

Missouri River

| Hastings' Cutoff |
| Donner Party Route |
| Oregon Trail |
| California Trail (Bidwell's Route) |

| 0 | 400 | 800 kilometers |
| 0 | 250 | 500 miles |

The Oregon Trail, a 2,000-mile (3,200 km) route that was first used exclusively by trappers, is seen in detail on this map. During the 1800s, settlers also used the Oregon Trail to head west. One of the most famous events that took place on the Oregon Trail was tragic. It involved the Donner Party, a group of eighty-seven pioneers who were trapped by snow near what is now the California-Nevada border. The Donner Party route and Hastings' Cutoff, where the party originally lost its way, are also shown.

Another well-worn trail during the 1840s was the Mormon Trail. Mormons are members of the Church of Jesus Christ of Latter-day Saints. Joseph Smith founded this group in 1830 in New York. However, Smith and the Mormons were driven out of New York and, later, out of Ohio, Missouri, and Illinois, where Smith died at the hands of an angry mob in Carthage. The Mormon Trail was different from the other trails because it was used by people fleeing religious persecution.

In February 1846, Brigham Young led the Mormons out of Illinois. Their route, the Mormon Trail, crossed the Missouri River in the

Great Plains. Then it followed the Oregon Trail to South Pass. Next it turned southwest. It ended in the valley of the Great Salt Lake in present-day Utah. Here, the Mormons made their final home. The first settlers arrived in July 1847, and as time passed, Mormons poured into the valley from eastern states and distant European countries. By 1860, the settlement, called Deseret, had 60,000 residents.

Other trails were the Bozeman Trail and the Gila Trail. John Bozeman blazed the Bozeman Trail in 1863 while searching for gold in the High Plains. This trail branched off the Oregon Trail on the east side of the Rocky Mountains. It went north and then west, ending in Virginia City, Nevada. Many Indian tribes such as the Crow, Sioux, and Cheyenne occupied the High Plains. Time after time, they drove out the gold seekers, and within five years, the Bozeman Trail fell out of use.

Although the Gila Trail was rugged, it got more use than the Bozeman Trail. The Gila Trail cut through the hot, dry regions of Texas, New Mexico, and Arizona. Once in California, it branched to reach Los Angeles and San Diego. Archaeologists believe that Native Americans used parts of the Gila Trail thousands of years ago. It also served early Spanish explorers, including

American religious leader Brigham Young (1801–1877) was a devout Mormon. His contributions to the Mormon Church helped the religion prosper after its followers were driven out of New York. Young is remembered as a pioneer whose contributions and leadership influenced the development of the American West.

Francisco Vásquez de Coronado in the 1540s.

Life and Death on the Trail

On the trail, pioneers trekked about 15 miles (24 km) per day, unless they were traveling over rough terrain, which slowed their progress. For example, crossing a swift river could take an entire day.

The pioneers traveled with mules and canvas-covered wagons shaped like long, shallow boats. When the wind blew, the canvas billowed. The wagons looked like ships on a sea of grass and were often called prairie schooners. (A schooner is a kind of boat.)

Families packed their wagons full of supplies for the long journey. A food supply commonly included 200 pounds (91 kg) of flour, 150 pounds (68 kg) of bacon, 10 pounds (4.5 kg) of coffee, 20 pounds (9.07 kg) of sugar, 10 pounds (4.5 kg) of salt, and many barrels of water. They also packed rope, spare wagon parts, furniture, and cooking pots. All of this made a heavy load. Still, they tucked in precious items such as china dishes, mirrors, and small keepsakes.

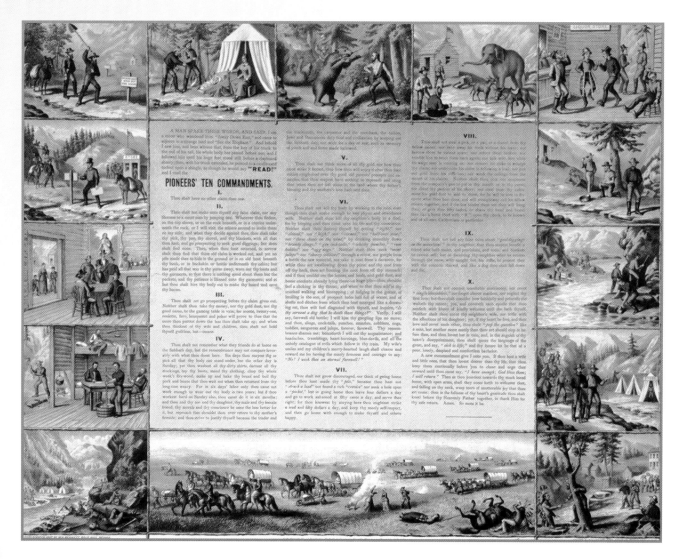

"The Miner's Pioneer Ten Commandments of 1849" features fourteen scenes of pioneer gold miners' lives, including camp life, attacks by Indians and bears, and crossing the plains. The text, which was originally published as a letter sheet (a single paper that folded into an envelope) in 1853 by James Mason Hutchings, sold more than 100,000 copies. It included such advice as "Thou shall have no other [mining] claim than one," and "Thou shall not steal a pick, a pan, or a shovel, from thy fellow miner."

On the trail, pioneers faced many dangers. Indian attacks were rare. The real threats were the rugged landscape and diseases. Rivers were wide, and there were no bridges. Pioneers drove wagons straight into the water. Mud swirled around the wheels and water rushed by with force. Quicksand pulled at livestock. Elsewhere, rocky ground shook the wagons, and the wheels often became loose or broken. Diseases such as smallpox, measles, pneumonia, and whooping cough all struck without warning. Perhaps the worst disease was cholera, which was often fatal in just a few hours.

Today, there are many records of the difficulties of pioneer life, including some of the hardships experienced by children. These accounts were often kept in journals. In 1846, eleven-year-old Lucy Henderson Deady wrote about her younger sister, Salita Jane, who drank an entire bottle of medicine and died of the overdose. Another diary tells the story of Catherine Sager, age thirteen, who fell under the wagon wheels in 1847, which crushed her left leg. In 1849, all the children in the Haun family were injured in a buffalo stampede. Sometimes children got lost on the trail and were never found. Such is the story of Amelia Stewart Knight.

The tragedy of one group shocked many. The Donner Party had eighty-seven men, women, and children who left Missouri on the Oregon Trail in the spring of 1846. Their destination was California. Bad, rainy weather, thick underbrush, and desert heat slowed them down. Their oxen grew tired and died, and Indians stole their other livestock. The Donner Party was already tired, but soon they grew thirsty and cold, too. People argued and fought. By the time they had reached South Pass, winter had come. The party sent a small group to get help. Before help arrived, forty-one people had died. Starving survivors ate the flesh of the dead. Their tragedy is one example of the dangers of taming the West.

CHAPTER FIVE

Fighting over Slavery

Government leaders closely watched the settlement of the frontier. Between 1840 and 1860, seven new states formed. The leaders debated about whether these newly formed states should allow slavery. They fought over whether new states should be added to the nation as slave states or free states, which outlawed slavery. Disagreement over slavery was a major cause of the American Civil War (1861–1865). Most Southerners believed in the right to own slaves, while the majority of Northerners believed slavery should be abolished, or stopped.

In the North, slavery was less important to the economy. Farms used paid labor. Later, manufacturing became more common than farming. In manufacturing, products were made from raw materials, and machines did most of the work. Northerners got jobs working these machines, and they built and repaired them. Others sold the manufactured items such as clothing, shoes, and lumber. The Southern economy was different. In the South, slaves ran plantation farming.

Trying to Prevent War

At first, the North and the South tried to prevent war. They made agreements, including the Missouri Compromise (1820), the Compromise of 1850, and the Kansas-Nebraska Act (1854).

In 1819, there was a balance of eleven slave states and eleven free states. When Missouri applied to become a state, however, Northern and Southern representatives argued about whether Missouri should allow slavery. In 1820, the representatives agreed on the Missouri Compromise, allowing Missouri admission to the Union as a slave state. It was also agreed that Maine would be admitted as a free state. In addition, no new slave states would be made from the Louisiana Territory north of Missouri.

In 1849, California asked to be admitted as a free state, but Southern representatives opposed its admission without slavery. To

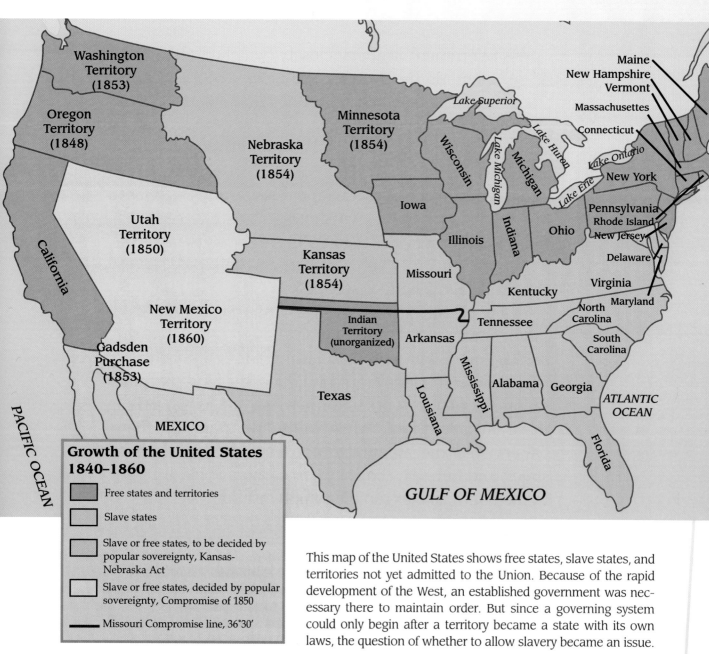

Growth of the United States 1840–1860

- Free states and territories
- Slave states
- Slave or free states, to be decided by popular sovereignty, Kansas-Nebraska Act
- Slave or free states, decided by popular sovereignty, Compromise of 1850
- Missouri Compromise line, 36°30'

This map of the United States shows free states, slave states, and territories not yet admitted to the Union. Because of the rapid development of the West, an established government was necessary there to maintain order. But since a governing system could only begin after a territory became a state with its own laws, the question of whether to allow slavery became an issue.

solve this problem Senator Henry Clay created the Compromise of 1850 in which California joined the nation as a free state. Slavery was abolished in the District of Columbia. The compromise also affected the New Mexico and Utah Territories. It said these citizens could decide for themselves whether to have slaves.

In 1854, the Kansas-Nebraska Act set up two new territories. In one way, this act was also a compromise. It allowed Kansas and Nebraska to decide for themselves whether to allow slavery. But these territories were in the Louisiana Territory. Under the Missouri Compromise, no slave states could be made there. The Kansas-Nebraska Act cancelled the Missouri Compromise. Many Americans reacted with disbelief and anger. This decision pushed the nation closer to civil war.

The Road to War

People opposing slavery were called abolitionists. Abolitionists made speeches against slavery and sometimes hid runaway slaves. They pleaded with slaveholders to give up using slave labor to run their plantations.

Some abolitionists helped slaves escape on the Underground Railroad, a series of safe houses along an escape route north. These routes ran through fourteen Northern states. They led slaves to Northern cities and Canada.

In 1852, Harriet Beecher Stowe published *Uncle Tom's Cabin.* This book showed the cruelness of slavery. By 1861, the book had sold 3 million copies, mostly in the North, where the majority of people agreed that slavery was cruel and unjust. However, Southern plantation owners demanded to keep slavery. As proof of their conviction, they threatened to secede (split) from the Union.

Then, in 1860, Abraham Lincoln, a Republican, won the presidential election. The Republicans were

The lithograph shown here, *The Sale of Uncle Tom at the Slave Market* first appeared in *Uncle Tom's Cabin,* an 1852 book by Harriet Beecher Stowe. Stowe's book incited many arguments against slavery, though it was most popular in the North where the majority of people wished to abolish the practice throughout the United States.

against slavery. Southern states did not want Lincoln as their president. One by one, they seceded from the Union. They formed the Confederate States of America under their own president, Jefferson Davis. The states of the Confederacy were South Carolina, Mississippi, Florida, Alabama, Georgia, Louisiana, Virginia, Texas, North Carolina, Tennessee, and Arkansas.

Civil War

Confederates fired the first shots of the Civil War at Fort Sumter, South Carolina, on April 12, 1861. Over the next four years, more than 843,000 Americans died in battle and from disease. At first, both sides thought the war would be short.

The first major battle was at Bull Run, a stream in Virginia. Union troops were on their way to attack Richmond, the Confederate capital. On July 21, 1861, they clashed with Confederate troops. General Thomas Jackson stood against Union forces like a stone wall, which earned him the nickname Stonewall Jackson. The Confederates drove the Union soldiers back to Washington.

At the Second Battle of Bull Run, Generals Jackson and James Longstreet commanded Confederate forces. General John Pope led Union troops. This battle lasted many months. Finally, on August 29 and 30, 1862, the Confederates drove Union troops back to Washington. This victory opened a path to the north. Confederate General Robert E. Lee led troops along this route.

In southwestern Tennessee, the Battle of Shiloh broke out on April 6, 1862. Here, Confederate troops took Union troops by surprise. Confederates under General Albert S. Johnston drove Union forces back. General Ulysses S. Grant, the Union commander, was shocked. But the next day, 25,000 more Union soldiers arrived. They forced a Confederate retreat. Thousands of soldiers on both sides died.

The war continued. Battles were fierce. The Battle of Antietam (1862) in Maryland was especially bloody. In one day of fighting, more soldiers were killed or wounded than on any other day in American history. Other major battles were at Fredericksburg, Virginia; Chancellorsville, Virginia; Vicksburg, Mississippi; Gettysburg, Pennsylvania; and Chattanooga, Tennessee. The North and the South each had days of victory and days of defeat. Finally, on April 9, 1865, General Lee surrendered to General Grant. The Civil War was over. The Union army had won.

Slaves were declared free even before the war ended. On January 1, 1863, President Lincoln issued the Emancipation Proclamation, a

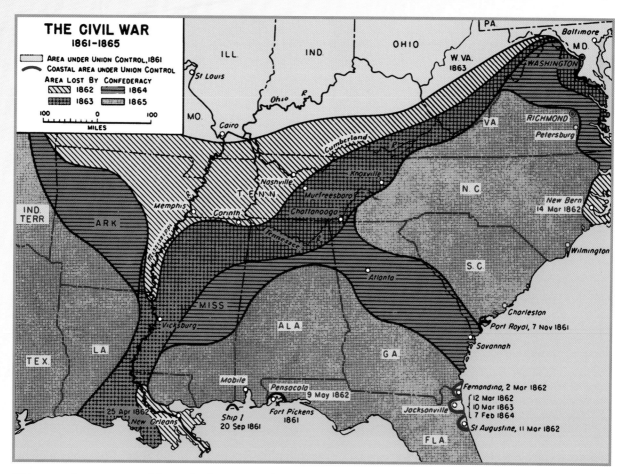

THE CIVIL WAR
1861-1865

☐ Area under Union Control, 1861
⌒ Coastal area under Union Control
Area Lost by Confederacy
▨ 1862   ▦ 1864
▦ 1863   ▧ 1865

This map shows areas of the United States under the control of Union (Northern) states and areas that were lost by the Confederacy (Southern) states during the time of the American Civil War. Thousands of lives were lost battling over the issue of slavery and the future of America. Finally, on April 9, 1865, Confederate troops under General Robert E. Lee surrendered to Union forces.

declaration that announced that all slaves in the Confederacy were free. Then, in 1865, the Thirteenth Amendment to the Constitution was ratified (approved). The passage of the Thirteenth Amendment officially abolished slavery.

Lincoln also began Reconstruction, which was a plan to rebuild the South. After Lincoln, President Andrew Johnson continued the rebuilding. Johnson officially pardoned former Confederate citizens.

This means he legally forgave them for their part in the war.

During Reconstruction, federal troops occupied the South. These states were adjusting to a nonslave economy. The troops established new governments. They founded The Bureau of Refugees, Freedmen, and Abandoned Lands in 1865, an association meant to help freed slaves. Lawmakers also passed the Civil Rights Act of 1866 and ratified the Fourteenth Amendment in 1868,

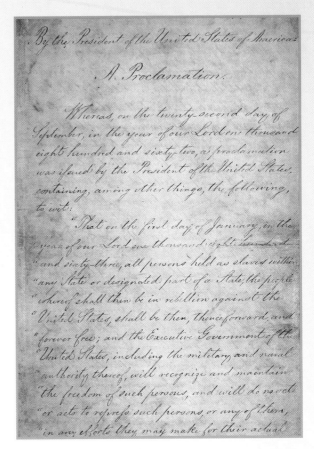

Abraham Lincoln (1809–1865), who served as the sixteenth president of the United States from 1861 until his assassination in 1865, is pictured in this daguerreotype, a kind of early photograph. Lincoln is remembered as the "Great Emancipator" since his leadership helped end slavery in the United States. His famous decree, the Emancipation Proclamation *(right),* which announced that "all persons held as slaves within the rebellious areas [Confederate states] are, and henceforward shall be free," was first issued on September 22, 1862.

which gave citizenship to all blacks. In 1870, the Fifteenth Amendment gave black men the right to vote.

The Northern states thought that President Johnson was not strict enough. They wanted the South to be punished. Then Johnson fired the U.S. secretary of war, Edwin M. Stanton. Stanton had helped lead the North to victory. In response, the House of Representatives voted to impeach President Johnson. This means they charged him with misconduct in office. They pointed out

the Tenure of Office Act. Because of this law Congress claimed that Johnson did not have the right to fire Stanton. The case went to trial before the Senate in 1868. However, the Senate failed to convict Johnson, and he finished his term.

After the war, former slave owners were unhappy with their new way of life. In 1865 and 1866, Southern states made laws known as the black codes. Under these laws, blacks were treated as lower members of society. Race riots broke out in Southern cities. In

This illustration depicts activities during the 1866 New Orleans race riot, a massacre of human lives that occurred when former Confederates attacked a congressional convention in Louisiana. President Andrew Johnson and the mayor of New Orleans were also implicated in the conflict that killed 34 African Americans and three white radicals. *Harper's Weekly* published this illustration around the time of the riot.

the New Orleans race riot in 1866, 100 persons were injured, and 34 blacks and three whites were killed.

Racial problems continued throughout Reconstruction, which ended in 1877. At this time, the last federal troops pulled out of the South. After Reconstruction, Southern states passed Jim Crow laws. These laws legalized racial segregation—separation based on race. Because of these laws, people were segregated according to the color of their skin. In an effort to prevent blacks from being equal in their status to whites, both races were segregated in schools, parks, on public transportation, in theaters, and in restaurants. In 1954 the Supreme Court declared segregation in public schools unconstitutional. The Jim Crow laws were made unlawful after the Civil Rights Act of 1964. Even so, racial conflicts throughout the United States still exist today.

CHAPTER SIX
Settling the West

"Go West, young man, and grow up with the country" wrote L. B. Soule, a nineteenth-century newspaper editor. At the time, pioneers were rushing to the trails leading west. By 1864, this inspiring statement found its way into print again. This time, Horace Greeley used it in an editorial in the *New York Times,* and it was read by millions of Americans.

The Homestead Act of 1862 encouraged Americans to settle the frontier by giving them land in exchange for a small fee. They had to live on and improve the land for five years. A typical land grant was about 160 acres (65 ha). Thousands of families got their start with this system. In addition, land speculators grabbed up land parcels and sold them to homesteaders or other speculators. By 1900, 600,000 homesteaders

Secretary of War Jefferson Davis commissioned this 1858 United States map that illustrates territory from the Mississippi River west to the Pacific Ocean. The map surveyed the land and included a report about Indian tribal locations, military posts, and areas suitable for the construction of railroads. Davis, who was elected president of the Confederate States of America in 1861, had a long history of holding various government offices, including terms in both the House of Representatives and the Senate.

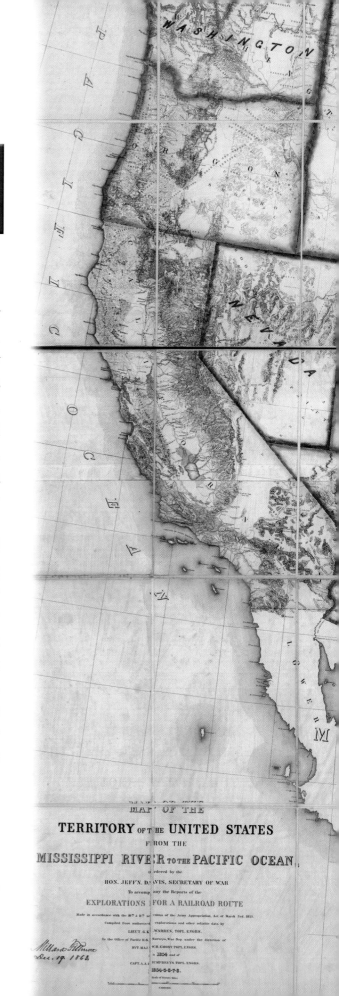

MAP OF THE
TERRITORY OF THE **UNITED STATES**
FROM THE
MISSISSIPPI RIVER TO THE **PACIFIC OCEAN**,
ordered by the
HON. JEFF'N. DAVIS, SECRETARY OF WAR
To accompany the Reports of the
EXPLORATIONS FOR A RAILROAD ROUTE

had claimed more than 80 million acres (32 million ha) under this law.

Pioneer Lifestyles

Pioneers had to make new lives from scratch. Food and shelter were their main needs. Unlike people in eastern cities, pioneers had to live off the land. To grow crops, they first had to cultivate the land, which was back-breaking work. A new invention, the steel plow, helped. Common crops were corn, wheat, and beans. Other food was wild game—deer, birds, and buffalo. Some farms also had pigs, chickens, and cows.

Pioneers built homes from natural materials. For cabins, they used logs about 16 to 18 feet (4.9 to 5.5 meters) long. They stacked the logs for walls. Wood chips and mud or clay sealed the cracks. Other homes were made of blocks of sod (earth). Pioneers stacked sod bricks for walls. Sometimes they dug into the side of a hill to form a sod house.

A pioneer family poses in front of their covered wagon in Loup Valley, Nebraska, while on their way to their new home. The Homestead Act of 1862 allowed any citizen over the age of twenty-one to claim 160 acres (65 ha) for the price of a filing fee, provided they improved it and lived on it for at least five years.

Every member of a pioneer family had to work hard. Men and older boys farmed and hunted. They defended their families during fights with Native Americans. Younger boys ground corn and tended farm animals. Women and girls cooked meals. They made cornbread, biscuits, and flapjacks. They also made clothing and cared for younger children.

Although each new settlement had its own school, books were scarce. Because of this, the schoolteacher gave lessons aloud. In this way, students learned by memorizing information. In 1862, Congress passed the Morrill Act, which gave public lands to each state. States sold this land and used the income to build colleges. They became known as land-grant colleges or "A&M" (agriculture and manufacturing) colleges.

The Morrill Act of 1862, named in honor of its sponsor, Vermont congressman Justin Smith Morrill, helped establish colleges throughout the United States to teach agriculture and mechanical arts. Under the law, each state was granted 30,000 acres (12,141 ha) of federal land for each member of Congress representing that state. The schools were then established with money earned from the sale of the donated land.

Gold!

In 1848, James Marshall discovered gold in the California Territory. He was building a sawmill for his boss, John Sutter, and found a small gold nugget in a ditch. The news of his discovery spread. Gold fever struck the rest of the country. Eighty thousand fortune seekers rushed to California by 1849. They were nicknamed "forty-niners." During the next four years, 250,000 more gold seekers arrived. Mining camps were established overnight. Many miners

These miners in Rockerville, South Dakota washed and panned gold in 1899, hoping to gain their fortune. Entire pioneer families headed west in search of gold and land in the 1840s and 1850s. Within a decade, precious minerals in the western United States became exhausted as mining operations grew into businesses that stripped the land of its minerals.

were small-time criminals, outlaws, gamblers, army deserters, and adventurers. With this mix of people, lawlessness grew.

The fortune seekers flocked to gold fields. These places took on names such as Whiskey Bark, Poker Flat, and Skunk Gulch. In 1852 alone, more than $81 million in gold was mined. Prices for food and other goods soared. New towns had sprung up suddenly. Because people couldn't survive without food and other necessities, merchants charged outrageous prices.

In 1858, gold was found west of Pikes Peak. The next year, gold and silver were found in Nevada. Here, the Comstock Lode and other gold mines yielded $100 million in ten years. Other gold and silver mines sprang up in Montana, Arizona, and South Dakota.

At first, gold dust and nuggets seemed plentiful. A man might find several hundred dollars' worth in a day. But as more people poured into the gold fields, the precious metal became harder to find. Organizations began taking over the work. They used machines to mine gold. Soon, many mining towns became ghost towns, while a few other towns survived. In these, law enforcement officers established governments. By 1875, the gold rush was over.

Transportation and Communication

The gold rush brought waves of new settlers to the territories. Soon California had enough inhabitants to apply for statehood. In 1850, California became a state. Now, the nation had states on each coast. By 1867, six more states formed. These included Kansas, Minnesota, Nebraska, Nevada, Oregon, and West Virginia.

Stagecoaches like those used by the Butterfield Overland Mail Company carried mail across the country. The cross-country trip took about twenty-five days. The Pony Express delivered mail faster by horseback. In this way, mail crossed the country in about ten days. Pony Express riders were teenage boys. William F. "Buffalo Bill" Cody was one of the most famous.

In 1860, railways linked eastern cities with more than 30,000 miles (48,280 km) of track. In 1862, President Lincoln signed the Pacific Railroad Act. It made plans for a

William F. "Buffalo Bill" Cody (1846–1917) earned his nickname after claiming to have single-handedly killed more than 4,000 buffalo in his lifetime. Cody was a rider for the Pony Express, a soldier in the Union army, and an actor in the traveling show that made him famous: Buffalo Bill's Wild West and Congress of Rough Riders of the World.

transcontinental railroad. On the West Coast, the Pacific Central rail line started in Sacramento, California, and reached the Nebraska Territory. Thousands of Chinese immigrants helped build it. The rail line from the east was the Union Pacific line, which was mostly built by Irish immigrants. On May 10, 1869, the two tracks met in Promontory, Utah.

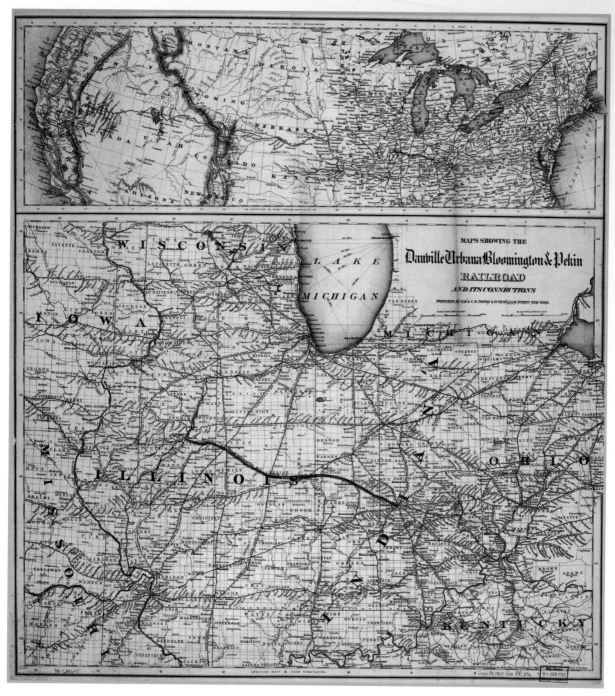

The Danville, Urbana, Bloomington, and Pekin Railroad and its connections are shown on this map of the midwestern United States. The rail line took three years to build and was opened to the public in 1869, the same year this map was created. Eventually it merged with another rail line to form the Indianapolis, Bloomington, and Western Railroad Company. The last passenger trains passed through Urbana, Illinois, in 1959.

Soon, other rail lines ran across the country, including the Southern Pacific, the Atchison, the Topeka, and the Santa Fe. Towns sprang up along the railroads. For Native Americans, the new railroads were destructive. The lines cut into their hunting grounds. Millions of buffalo were slaughtered. The Indians' way of life was seriously harmed.

During the 1860s, telegraph lines crisscrossed the country, too. In 1838, Samuel F. B. Morse sent the first telegraph in the United States. After that, companies stretched telegraph wires between cities. The telegraph was sometimes called the "talking" or "singing" wire. In 1851, Hiram Sibley formed the Western Union Telegraph Company.

The federal government wanted to connect the east and west by telegraph. Congress passed the Telegraph Act of 1860. It gave public lands and a contract to Sibley, who then formed the Pacific Telegraph Company. It built telegraph lines between Omaha, Nebraska, and Salt Lake City, Utah. This was the eastern portion. Sibley also formed the Overland Telegraph

The young men in this 1908 photograph were messenger boys working the night shift at the Western Union Telegraph Company, in Indianapolis, Indiana. According to statistics tabulated by the U.S. Department of Labor, more than 1,750,000 children were employed in the United States in 1900. The Western Union Telegraph Company formed in 1851, one decade before the first transcontinental line was created.

Company, which built the western portion of the telegraph line. It stretched from California to Salt Lake City. Here, the two lines met. On October 24, 1861, the first transcontinental message was transmitted over the wires.

Cowboys and Cattle Drives

Along with railroads and telegraphs, cowboys came to the frontier. They rode horseback, tending hundreds of longhorns in the Great Plains. Each spring, they drove herds to market, which supplied beef to cities across America. At first, cowboys drove the cattle to Chicago, where the animals were butchered. The raw beef was then delivered to consumers.

After the railroads were established, cattle could be shipped rapidly to eastern and western cities. Cowboys herded cattle to rail stations in "cow towns," which dotted Kansas, Texas, New Mexico, Colorado, Nebraska, and Missouri. These towns were usually rough and dangerous. Sheriffs and marshals tried to keep law and order. Some of these famous lawmen

Cowboys on horseback in this 1912 panoramic photograph of the American Southwest are rounding up cattle. Cowboys were responsible for keeping the cattle together and guiding them to pasture. They protected the animals, branded them, drove them to various shipping points, and confined them using barbed-wire fencing.

were Wyatt Earp, "Wild Bill" Hickok, and Bat Masterson.

The long routes to cow towns became well-traveled cattle trails. Most trails ran north and south. Major cattle trails were the Shawnee Trail, Chisholm Trail, Western Trail, Goodnight-Loving Trail, and Story Trail. The busiest years of the "cattle kingdom" were from the 1860s to the 1880s.

Two innovations helped cattle ranchers. These were barbed wire and deep-well drilling. Ranchers fenced off huge sections of land with barbed wire, which has sharp points set along it. They kept their herds together inside these barbed-wire fences. Sometimes ranchers fenced in public land or a neighbor's land, too. Many disagreements arose over fences. Ranchers argued, cut one another's fences, and even shot at one another. Between 1875 and 1880, millions of pounds of barbed wire were sold. Fenced-in herds also needed their own watering holes, which were created with deep-well drilling.

In the late 1880s, prices for beef fell. Then, terrible droughts and blizzards killed thousands of cattle. Ranchers went bankrupt. In addition, most of the land was now fenced off

James Butler "Wild Bill" Hickok (1837–1876) was an American frontiersman, marksman, U.S. marshal, and Union army scout during the Civil War. He became acquainted with Buffalo Bill when he toured with Buffalo Bill's Wild West Show from 1872 to 1873. Hickok was fatally shot while playing poker in Deadwood, South Dakota.

by ranchers. The cattle trails were no longer usable. The Wild West had been explored, settled, and fenced.

CHAPTER SEVEN
The End of an Era

In 1869, Ulysses S. Grant became president of the United States and served two consecutive terms from 1869 to 1877. Grant had gained fame in the Civil War, in which he had fought to preserve the Union. During his presidency, Grant saw the frontier ending. He wanted to preserve America's landscape. In 1872, Congress established Yellowstone National Park. It covered 3,468 square miles (8,982 sq km) in parts of Wyoming, Montana, and Idaho.

Cities and Social Classes

Until the Civil War, most Americans farmed or traded goods to survive. Slowly, U.S. cities grew in size and population. New England became industrialized, and people worked in factories. They produced goods by machine instead of by hand.

Yellowstone National Park is pictured in detail on this map from 1880. President Ulysses Grant declared the 2.2 million acre (890,308 ha) area a national park in 1872, and it became the first of its kind in the world. By 1895, more than 5,000 people visited the park annually for its beautiful vistas and natural geysers. Old Faithful, along with many other of the park's geysers, intermittently sends jets of heated water and steam into the air.

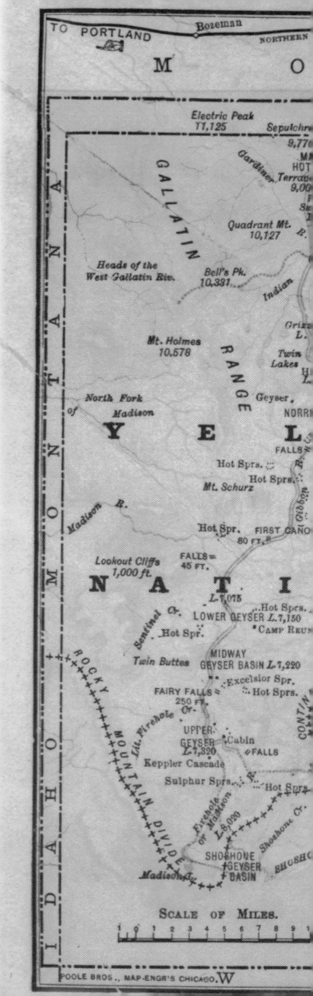

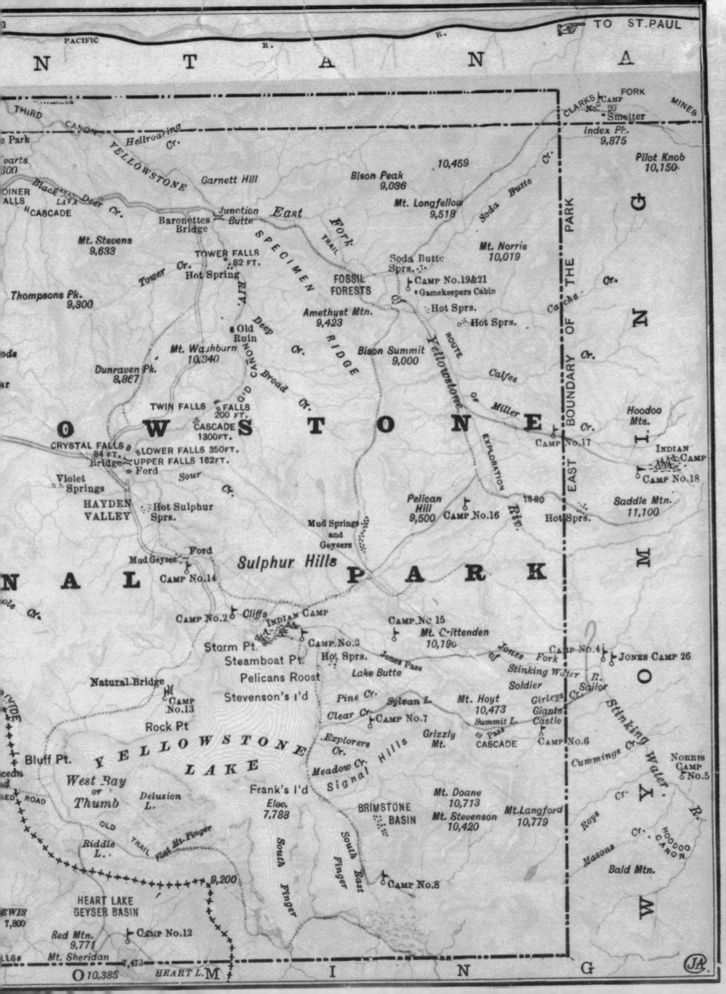

Then towns developed in the new territories. Mining towns were established and cow towns served the needs of ranchers. Railway stations became centers of activity.

Population growth allowed a greater division of labor as people specialized in different types of work. Blacksmiths forged metals, mill workers ground grain into flour, retailers sold clothing, and farmers harvested crops.

In cities, social classes took shape. The upper classes had the most wealth and were made up of families who often owned mills and factories. Other families inherited their wealth. The middle class included shopkeepers, businesspeople, and farmers. At the lowest level, the working class held the lowest-paying jobs in mines, factories, and railroads.

Factories like this one, J. O. Whitehouse's Boot and Shoe Factory in Poughkeepsie, New York, appeared throughout the northeast as manufacturing grew during the nineteenth century. New inventions, an eager work force, and a high demand for goods helped the United States become an industrialized nation.

During this period, inventors were hard at work. Many factory machines were designed in the 1800s, including steam-powered spinning machines, mechanical looms, sewing machines, and mechanical reapers for farming. The United States was quickly becoming an industrialized nation.

Government and Politics

Sixteen presidents led the United States between 1801 and 1877. Under their leadership, the nation expanded as presidents acquired new land. Congress appointed leaders for the territories who created state laws. With 5,000 citizens, a territory could elect its own legislature. With 60,000 citizens, a territory could apply to become a state.

Jefferson and the three presidents who followed him (James Madison, James Monroe, and John Quincy Adams) were Democratic-Republicans. This party did not support a strong federal government. Instead, it favored states' rights. During the 1820s, the Democratic-Republican Party split. One part became the National Republicans. They supported nationalism, a national bank, and certain tariffs (taxes). The other part became the Democratic Party. It supported states' rights, an independent treasury, and limited tariffs. Andrew Jackson led the Democrats. He was elected president in 1828 and again in 1832. This political party became the Democratic Party of today.

As president, Jackson made decisions that caused an economic depression. At that time, all government money was placed in the Bank of the United States. Jackson's supporters claimed this bank was too powerful. In response, Jackson moved all government money to smaller banks.

But Jackson's plan backfired. The smaller banks issued lots of paper money. They gave loans to land speculators. Also, the plentiful paper money caused inflation, or the rising of prices. Jackson tried to slow inflation. He said people must pay gold or silver for government land. People rushed to change paper money into gold or silver. Banks soon ran out of precious metals, and people panicked. Just at this time, Jackson left office. His successor, Martin Van Buren, had to manage the Panic of 1837.

A financial crisis is illustrated in this 1832 drawing titled "The Downfall of Mother Bank," which shows President Andrew Jackson (second from right) refusing to renew the charter of the Bank of the United States. Jackson instead chose to remove all government funds from the bank and deposit them in state banks around the country.

During Jackson's terms in office, the Whig Party formed. In part, it was made up of the National Republican Party. It included other groups that did not support Jackson. Whig presidents were William Henry Harrison, John Tyler, Zachary Taylor, and Millard Fillmore. In the 1850s, the Whig Party split over the issue of slavery. Most Southern Whigs supported slavery and joined the Democratic Party. Most Northern Whigs were against slavery. They joined with antislavery Democrats. Together, these two groups formed the Republican Party, which is still in existence.

President Lincoln was the first Republican president. In 1864, Union citizens elected Lincoln to a second term, but he was assassinated five days after the Civil War ended. Andrew Johnson, a Democrat, completed Lincoln's term in office. Republicans then became the dominant political party in the United States until roughly the 1930s.

Like Van Buren, Ulysses S. Grant was president during a depression that began as the Panic of 1873. "Greenback" paper money had been issued during the Civil War, but it was not backed by gold or silver in the federal treasury. As a result, greenbacks were worth less and less. Prices for goods and services rose. In

Investors clamor as officials close the doors of the New York Stock Exchange during the Panic of 1873. The term "panic" is used in economics to describe a disturbance in the world economy. Financial panics can cause banks to fail, investors to over-speculate, and stock markets to crash. The Panic of 1873 was the result of a long-term expansion in the world economy that dated back to the 1840s.

1875, Grant signed the Specie Resumption Act. It allowed greenbacks to be exchanged for gold or silver. Despite this measure, the depression stretched throughout Grant's second term in office.

The End of an Era

By the 1870s, the industrialized United States had finished growing in land size (at least until Hawaii became a U.S. territory in 1900). Its government and politics had gone through great changes, including the

Thousands of American settlers rush on to the Cherokee Strip in Oklahoma in September 1893 when the territory was opened to colonization. Most Americans held strong to the idea of manifest destiny at this time. Nineteenth-century "can-do" attitudes, the open landscape, free or low-cost land, new rail lines, and the promise of fruitful lifestyles made the difficult move westward seem romantic in the hearts and minds of many pioneers.

formation of a two-party political system. For Native Americans, an entire way of life had ended.

Today, the American imagination is rich with images of the frontier, the Wild West, and Native American culture. Frontier towns represent an untamed era. The plight of the Indians that was brought on by the physical growth of the United States represents a turbulent time in our nation's history. Reminders of traditional Indian culture are bittersweet because they recall the Native American struggle against greed and racism.

The idea of manifest destiny, of the American God-given right to claim land, sparked the transition of the United States into one of the world's strongest and wealthiest nations.

TIMELINE

1801 President Thomas Jefferson takes office.

1803 The United States pays France $15 million for the Louisiana Territory.

1804 On May 14, the Lewis and Clark expedition sets out from Missouri.

1811 On November 7, William Henry Harrison defeats the Prophet at the Battle of Tippecanoe.

1812 The War of 1812, between the United States and Great Britain, begins.

1814 The Treaty of Ghent ends the War of 1812.

1820 Congress approves the Missouri Compromise.

1821 William Becknell blazes the Santa Fe Trail.

1823 President Monroe presents the Monroe Doctrine.

1825 James Ohio Pattie blazes the Gila Trail.

1830 Congress passes the Indian Removal Act.

1835 The First Seminole War begins in Florida Territory.

1836 Mexican president Santa Anna attacks Texans at the Battle of the Alamo. On May 14, the Republic of Texas wins its independence from Mexico.

1837 President Van Buren copes with a financial panic.

1838 The U.S. Army forms the Corps of Topographical Engineers. In October, the Cherokee Indians begin the march known as the Trail of Tears.

1843 The Oregon Trail opens.

1845 John L. O'Sullivan coins the term "manifest destiny." Brigham Young leads the Mormons over the Mormon Trail.

1846 On May 11, President Polk declares war on Mexico. On June 15, the United States and Great Britain sign the Oregon Treaty.

1848 On January 24, James Marshall discovers gold at Sutter's Mill in California. On February 2, the Treaty of Guadalupe Hidalgo ends the Mexican-American War.

1849 The California gold rush begins.

1850 The Compromise of 1850 addresses slavery in new territories.

1853 The Gadsden Purchase adds the final territory to the contiguous United States.

1860 Abraham Lincoln wins the presidential election.

1861 Confederates fire the first shots of the Civil War at Fort Sumter, South Carolina. The first cross-country telegraph message is sent.

1862 Congress passes the Homestead Act.

1863 John Bozeman blazes the Bozeman Trail. President Lincoln issues the Emancipation Proclamation.

1865 On April 9, the Civil War ends with General Lee's surrender to General Grant. The Thirteenth Amendment passes, abolishing slavery.

1866 The first big cattle drives begin in Texas. Congress passes the Civil Rights Act.

1867 The United States buys Alaska from Russia for $7,200,000.

1869 The transcontinental railroad is completed.

1870 The Fifteenth Amendment , allowing blacks to vote, is passed.

1872 Yellowstone National Park is created.

1873 The country undergoes another financial panic.

abolish To cause to end.

acquire To get or take possession of.

annex To add something (such as land) to something larger (such as a country).

compromise An agreement reached when both sides give up some desires.

contiguous Touching. The United States has forty-eight contiguous states.

corps An organized group, often a military group.

depression A period of economic decline.

emancipate To free from oppression, slavery, or restraint.

expansion Growth; spreading out.

frontier Unsettled land along the edge of settled land.

Gadsen Purchase A controversial transaction made by James Gadsen to purchase a strip of land from Mexico in 1852.

Great Plains The west-central plains of the United States, east of the Rocky Mountains.

immigrant A person who moves from his/her country of birth to another country.

impeach To bring an accusation against, especially a president.

Indian Removal Act A law that was passed by Congress in 1830 that allowed President Andrew Jackson to forcibly move thousands of Native Americans from their eastern homes to lands west of the Mississippi River.

manifest destiny The idea that Americans had the God-given right to spread across the continent.

missionary A person sent by a religious group. He or she usually starts a church and/or school.

Monroe Doctrine A message delivered by President James Monroe in 1823, in which he asserted that Americans would stay out of European affairs.

Native Americans Also called Indians. The original peoples of North America. They were here long before Europeans arrived.

pioneer A person who is among the first to settle a region.

reconstruction The process of building again. After the Civil War, the South went through a time of reconstruction.

secede To withdraw from a union.

specie Money in coin form.

speculator A person who buys land and hopes that it grows more valuable. The goal is to resell it at a profit.

territory Land claimed by a nation.

Trail of Tears A term used to describe the forced march of the Cherokee Indians to lands west of the Mississippi River in the 1830s.

transcontinental Crossing the entire continent or country.

Treaty of Guadalupe Hidalgo An agreement signed in 1848 at the end of the Mexican-American War. Its main provision called for Mexico to give up much of its territory in exchange for American war reparations.

Wild West In the nineteenth century, unsettled frontier land in the western United States.

FOR MORE INFORMATION

Black American West Museum and
 Heritage Center
3091 California Street
Denver, CO 80205
(303) 292-2566
Web site: http://www.
 blackamericanwest.org

Smithsonian National Museum of
 American History
14th Street and Constitution
 Avenue, NW
Washington, DC 20240

(202) 633-1000
Web site: http://americanhistory.si.edu

Web Sites

Due to the changing nature of Internet
links, the Rosen Publishing Group,
Inc., has developed an online list of
Web sites related to the subject of this
book. This site is updated regularly.
Please use this link to access the list:

http://www.rosenlinks.com/
 ushagn/ammd

FOR FURTHER READING

Collier, Christopher, and James
 Lincoln Collier. *Indians,
 Cowboys, and Farmers and
 the Battle for the Great Plains.*
 New York: Benchmark
 Books, 2001.
Sakurai, Gail. *Asian-Americans
 in the Old West.* New York:
 Children's Press, 2000.

Schlissel, Lillian. *Black Frontiers: A
 History of African American Heroes
 in the Old West.* New York:
 Aladdin, 2000.
Weber, Michael. *Civil War and
 Reconstruction.* Austin: Raintree
 Steck-Vaughn, 2001.
Uschan, Michael V. *Westward Expansion.*
 San Diego: Lucent Books, 2001.

BIBLIOGRAPHY

Collier, Christopher, and James
 Lincoln Collier. *Indians, Cowboys,
 and Farmers and the Battle for the
 Great Plains.* New York:
 Benchmark Books, 2001.
Hillstrom, Kevin, and Laurie
 Collier Hillstrom. *American
 Civil War Almanac.* Detroit: UXL
 Gale, 2000.
McLynn, Frank. *Wagons West: The Epic
 Story of America's Overland Trails.*
 New York: Grove Press, 2002.

Pendergrast, Tom, and Sara
 Pendergrast. *Westward Expansion
 Almanac.* Detroit: UXL Gale, 2000.
Schlissel, Lillian. *Women's Diaries of the
 Westward Journey.* Edited by Gerda
 Lerner. New York: Schocken
 Books, 1992.
Sherrow, Victoria. *Life During the
 Gold Rush.* San Diego: Lucent
 Books, 1998.
Uschan, Michael V. *Westward Expansion.*
 San Diego: Lucent Books, 2001.

INDEX

About the Author

Lesli J. Favor enjoys writing about people and events that have shaped North America. Her books include *Francisco Vásquez de Coronado*, *The Iroquois Constitution*, and *Martin Van Buren*. She lives in Dallas, Texas. This city was once a tiny settlement on the Shawnee Cattle Trail. She earned her B.A. in English at the University of Texas at Arlington. She earned her M.A. and Ph.D. from the University of North Texas.

Photo Credits

Cover (background), pp. 1, 12–13, 16, 17, 29, 44–45, 50, 54–55 Library of Congress, Geography and Map Division; cover (top and bottom) 6–7, 20 (top), 34, 35, 42 (left), 51, 52, 56 Library of Congress, Prints and Photographs Division; pp. 4–5 © Bettmann/Corbis; pp. 8–9, 24–25, 41 courtesy of the General Libraries, the University of Texas at Austin; pp. 10, 26 © National Portrait Gallery, Smithsonian Institution/Art Resource, NY; p. 11 (left and right) Independence National Historical Park; p. 14 © James L. Amos/Corbis; pp. 20 (bottom), 22, 43 © 2003 Picture History, LLC; pp. 21, 38 maps designed by Tahara Hasan; pp. 23, 46, 57, 58, 59 © Hulton/Archive/Getty Images; p. 28 (left and right) Treaty of Guadalupe Hidalgo. February 2, 1848, Perfected Treaties, 1778–1945; Record Group 11, General Records of the United States Government, 1178–1992, National Archives; pp. 30–31, 33 © Maps.com/Corbis; p. 39 © Historical Picture Archive/ Corbis; p. 42 (right) Emancipation Proclamation, January 1, 1863, Presidential Proclamations, 1791–1991, Record Group 11, General Records of the United States, National Archives; p. 47 Enrolled Acts and Resolutions of Congress, 1789–1996, Record Group 11, General Records of the United States Government, National Archives; p. 48 © Denver Public Library, Western History Collection, Louis Charles McClure, MCC-2869; p. 49 © Lake County Museum/Corbis; p. 53 © The Art Archive/National Archives, Washington, D.C.

Designer: Tahara Anderson; **Editor:** Joann Jovinelly